MICHAEL CARD

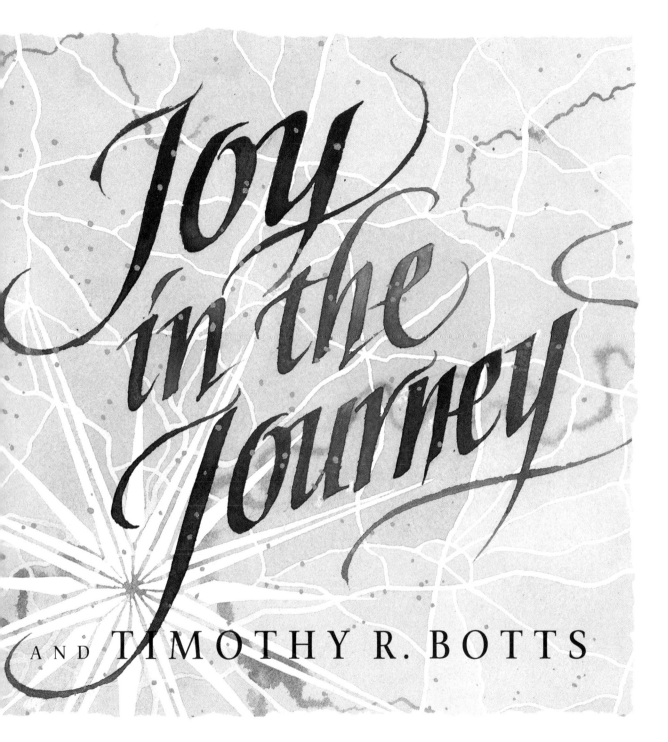

Joy in the Journey

AND TIMOTHY R. BOTTS

A JANET THOMA BOOK

THOMAS NELSON PUBLISHERS
Nashville Atlanta London Vancouver

Copyright © 1996 by Michael Card and Timothy R. Botts

Published in Nashville, Tennessee, by Thomas Nelson,
Inc., Publishers, and distributed in Canada by Word
Communications, Ltd., Richmond, British Columbia.

The Bible Version used in this publication is *The New
King James Version*. Copyright © 1979, 1980, 1982,
1990, Thomas Nelson, Inc., Publishers.

Library of Congress Cataloging-in-Publication Data

Card, Michael, 1957-
    Joy in the journey / Michael Card and Timothy Botts.
        p. cm.
    ISBN 0-7852-7789-7
    1. Christian Poetry, American. 2. Bible—History of Biblical
events—Poetry. I. Botts, Timothy R. II. Title.
PS3553.A654J69   1996
811'.54—dc20   96-6337
                                                                   CIP

Printed in the United States of America

1 2 3 4 5 6—01 00 99 98 97 96

*This book
is dedicated,
as a small
token of
encouragement,
to my wife,
Susan*

LONG AGO I realized that one purpose of the Bible was to turn an eye into an ear. "Pay careful attention to what you have *heard*," the writer of Hebrews warns his readers (2:1). The author intends for his readers to become *hearers* of the Word in the truest sense.

Music provides a means toward this transformation. I suppose that's what attracted me to songwriting in the first place. It offers another vehicle for experiencing what the Bible has to say. Another way to *hear*. And so for the past several years I have attempted to "pay careful attention to what I have heard" in the voice of Scripture and to put these truths into simple songs.

In a sense all real ministry is simply an attempt to help others hear what God is saying. In the hearing, ministry happens.

When I experience the work of Tim Botts my eyes become ears. Some of his illustrations crackle with energy and spirit. Others moan and wail, all the while causing something inside us to want to grieve as well. Still others sing with their own silent music, leading us to worship with a sort of hushed, wordless excitement. Seeing them helps us to better hear what God is trying to say.

So open your eyes and listen in a fresh new way to these songs which are products of listening in the first place. Then go back to the Bible—their true source—and "pay careful attention to what you hear."

M I C H A E L   C A R D

To my brothers
Gregory Jay
and
Kenneth Allen,
fellow artists
on the journey

WHEN I first heard Michael Card in concert I was drawn to his simple but poetic way of expressing deep truths. Relating so strongly to his lyrics, I jumped at the chance to give his music a visual dimension—to give these important life principles a face.

I enjoyed developing some new symbols for old truths. There is a rocking chair for God's acceptance of me and a lantern for my "joy in the journey." I expressed Jesus' name as a prismatic jewel and the words of God as flames from the Bible's pages. In order to represent the Lord's rising, I found myself immersed in a library book devoted to more than 18,000 species of butterflies. A Jewish friend helped familiarize me with the Hebrew alphabet for "El Shaddai."

Paradoxes of the Kingdom challenged my creativity: to be adopted by a king, the lamb who is a lion, freedom in the absence of possessions, and a fortune for fools. The act of making these pictures often turned into times of worship for me. I hope that in viewing them you too will revel in the King of Glory.

TIMOTHY R. BOTTS

CONTENTS

The story of Alpha and Omega from the

PART ONE

Love's Sacred Mystery

Torah's promise to the Gospels' fulfillment

THE BEGINNING (Genesis)

In the beginning was the Beginning
In Him it all began
All that they had was God and the garden
The woman and the man
Before Creation learned to groan
The stars would dance and sing
Each moment was new, every feeling was
    fresh
For the creature, king and queen

But deep in the heart of that beautiful
    garden
Forbidden fruit was found
And they were deceived, disobeyed and
    were driven
From that holy ground
But beside the tree of disobedience
The Tree of Life did grow
The gifts of its fruit an eternal beginning
But they would never know

The Beginning will make all things new
New Life belongs to Him
He hands us each new moment saying
My child, begin again
My child, begin again
You're free to start again

This very moment is filled with His power
That we might start anew
To break us away from the past and the
    future
He does what He must do
And so the Alpha brings to us this moment
    to commence
To live in the freedom of total forgiveness
With reckless confidence
With reckless confidence

In the beginning God created the heavens and
the earth. Genesis 1:1

***K**arl Barth, the Swiss theologian, said,
"It is not as important to begin as it is to
learn to begin again." And he was right.
Though our salvation was bought for us by
Jesus Christ, the actual *living out* of the
Christian life is a continuous process of
beginning again. Instead of condemning
us, the spirit of the Lord whispers, "Begin
again." This freedom is granted moment by
moment, each day of our lives.

THE ALPHA

BRINGS
TO US
THIS MOMENT
TO COMMENCE

to live in
the freedom of
total forgiveness

with
reckless
confidence

EL SHADDAI

El Shaddai, El Shaddai, El Elyon na Adonai,
Age to age You're still the same
By the power of the name
El Shaddai, El Shaddai, Erekamka na Adonai
We will praise and lift You high
El Shaddai

Through Your love and through the ram
You saved the son of Abraham
And by the power of Your hand
Turned the sea into dry land
To the outcast on her knees
You were the God who really sees
And by Your might You set Your children
   free

Through the years You made it clear
That the time of Christ was near
Though the people failed to see
What Messiah ought to be
Though Your Word contained the plan
They just could not understand
Your most awesome work was done
Through the frailty of Your Son

This song wrote itself. In the Old Testament we see God Almighty, El Shaddai. He parts oceans, sends plagues, and destroys pagan altars with fire. His arm is unimaginably strong. In the New Testament we have His Son who could not seem to be more different. Jesus is the meek, lamblike Savior, except for two incidents when he loses His temper in the temple court. He does not send His followers to die; He dies for them.

God, who is the same God in both testaments, is demonstrating His power. In the Old Testament He reveals the power of His might; in the New, He displays the power of His weakness. Through the human frailty of His only Son, God is showing the world what an absolutely awesome God He is. Once this idea was clear to me, the words of "El Shaddai" came in minutes.

El Shaddai
El Shaddai
El Elyon na Adonai
Age to age
You're still the same
By the power of the name
El Shaddai, El Shaddai
Erekamka na Adonai
We will praise
and lift you high
El Shaddai

HIS GOD (Job's Suite)

Who is it that darkens my counsel?
Who speaks empty words without
    knowledge?
Brace yourself up like a man
And answer me now, if you can

Can you put on glory and splendor?
What's the way to the home of the light?
Does your voice sound like the thunder?
Are you not afraid?
Where were you when earth's foundations
    were laid?

Who gave the heart its wisdom?
The mind its desire to know?
Can you bind the stars?
Raise your voice to the clouds?
Did you make the eagle proud?

Will the ox spend the night by your
    manger?
Did you let the wild donkey go free?
Can you take leviathan home as a pet?
If you merely touched him, you'd never
    forget.

Who is it that darkens my counsel?
Who speaks empty words without
    knowledge?
Brace yourself up like a man
And answer me now, if you can

HIS RESPONSE
I am unworthy, how can I reply?
There's nothing that you cannot do
You are the storm that calmed my soul
I place my hand over my mouth
I place my hand over my mouth

*J*ob's story is a parable as well as a true-life account. And so is your life and mine. If we find ourselves on the ash heap, full of angry questions, we need to prepare for an onslaught of silence.

The Lord will not always give us answers, but He will always give us Himself.

16

CAN YOU BIND THE STARS?

CAN YOU BIND THE STARS?

RAISE YOUR VOICE to the clouds?

Did you make the eagle proud?

THE MIND ITS DESIRE TO KNOW?

Who gave the heart its wisdom?

WHERE WERE YOU WHEN EARTH'S FOUNDATIONS WERE LAID?

I am unworthy, how can I reply?

THERE'S NOTHING THAT YOU CANNOT DO

You are the storm that calmed my soul

I place my hand over my mouth

THEY CALLED HIM LAUGHTER
(Isaac/Genesis 21)

A barren land
And a barren life
Made Abraham laugh
At his wandering life
A cruel joke it seemed then
To call him the "father of nations"

A heavenly prank?
A celestial joke?
'Cause grey hair and babies
Leave no room for hope
But hoping was something
This hopeless old man learned to do

They called him laughter
For he came after
The Father had made an
Impossible promise come true
The birth of a baby
To a hopeless old lady
So they called him laughter
'Cause no other name would do

A cry in the darkness
And laughter at night
An elderly couple sit
Holding him tight
An improbable infant
A punchline, a promise come true

They laughed till they wept
Then they laughed at their tears
This miracle baby they'd wanted for years
Would make a Messiah
Who'd give us impossible Joy

When God finally blessed Abraham and Sarah with a son, their laughter was because of disbelief. After all, who could believe such unbelievably good news?

Perhaps that is one reason their miracle son was named Isaac, which means laughter. Their home became a place of joy because God kept His promise and gave them a son.

they called him "LAUGHTER" FOR laughter HE CAME AFTER the father had made an impossible promise come true

the birth of a baby to a hopeless old lady

THE PROMISE

The Lord God said when time was full
He would shine His light in the darkness
He said a virgin would conceive[1]
And give birth to the Promise
For a thousand years the dreamers
Dreamt and hoped to see His love
But the Promise showed their wildest
   dreams
Had simply not been wild enough

The Promise was love
And the Promise was life
The Promise meant light to the world
Living proof that Yahweh saves
For the name of the Promise was Jesus

The Faithful One saw time was full
And the ancient pledge was honored
So God the Son the Incarnate One
His final Word His own Son
Was born in Bethlehem but came into our
Hearts to live
What more could God have given, tell me
What more did He have to give?

[1] Isaiah 7:14

God's promises are another way He gives Himself to us. They can be beautiful like a rainbow. Or fearful, like the promise of judgment. Either way, they are wonder-filled.

The greatest promise of all was the person God called "the Promised One." Through the promise of Jesus of Nazareth, God finally gave us all of Himself.

THE LORD GOD SAID
when time was full
He would shine His light in the darkness
He said a virgin would conceive
and give birth to the Promise
For a thousand years the dreamers dreamt
and hoped to see His love
But the Promise showed their wildest dreams
had simply not been wild enough
for the name of the Promise
is

IMMANUEL

A sign shall be given
A virgin will conceive[1]
A human baby bearing
Undiminished Deity
The glory of the nations [2]
A light for all to see
And hope for all who will embrace
His warm reality

Immanuel
Our God is with us [3]
And if our God is with us
Who could stand against us [4]
Our God is with us
Immanuel

For all those who live in the shadow of
    death
A glorious light has dawned [5]
For all those who stumble in darkness
Behold your light has come![6]

So what will be your answer?
Oh will you hear the call?
Of Him who did not spare His son
But gave him for us all
On earth there is no power
There is no depth or height
That could ever separate us from the love[7]
    of God in Christ

[1] Isaiah 7:14
[2] Psalms 96:3, 39:21
[3] Matthew 1:23
[4] Romans 8:31
[5] Isaiah 9:2
[6] Isaiah 60:1
[7] Romans 8:35

*"Therefore the Lord Himself will give you a
sign: Behold, the virgin shall conceive and
bear a Son, and shall call His name
Immanuel."* Isaiah 7:14

*L*ike most Old Testament names,
Immanuel was as much a description of
Jesus' life as a name. It was, in fact, more a
prophecy than a name, and more a
promise than a prophecy. *God with us.*
What an unimaginable reality—the
fullness of God in warm, human flesh!
With us. And more than that, for the life of
Jesus demonstrates that He is *for us!*

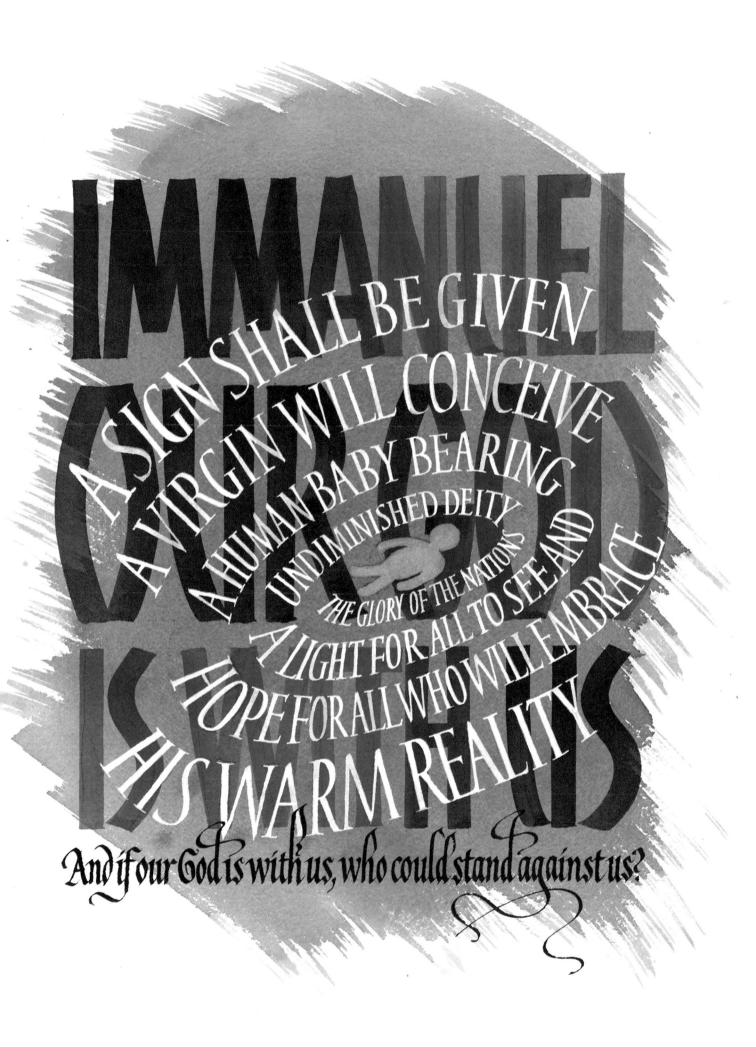

IMMANUEL

OUR GOD IS WITH US

A SIGN SHALL BE GIVEN
A VIRGIN WILL CONCEIVE
A HUMAN BABY BEARING
UNDIMINISHED DEITY
THE GLORY OF THE NATIONS
A LIGHT FOR ALL TO SEE AND
HOPE FOR ALL WHO WILL EMBRACE
HIS WARM REALITY

And if our God is with us, who could stand against us?

CELEBRATE THE CHILD

Celebrate the Child who is the Light
Now the darkness is over
No more wandering in the night
Celebrate the Child who is the Light

You know this is no fable
Godhead and manhood became one
We see He's more than able
And so we live in God the Son

Firstborn of creation[1]
Lamb and Lion, God and Man
The Author of Salvation
Almighty wrapped in swaddling bands

[1] Colossians 1:15

*T*he birth of any child is an occasion for celebration. How much more, then, the birth of *the* Child! On earth, though, celebration seems to be strangely absent. For the shepherds there was wonder; for the wise men, relief; for Joseph and Mary, a scene of desperation, poverty, and pain.

Worship was a part of all of their experiences, however. In wonder, in relief, and most especially in pain, our worship finds a beginning.

THE NAZARENE

The Nazarene had come to live the life of
    every man
And He felt the fascination of the stars
And as He wandered through this weary
    world
He wondered and He wept
For there were so few who'd listen to His
    call

He came, He saw, He surrendered all
So that we might be born again
And the fact of his humanity was there for all
    to see
For he was unlike any other man
And yet so much like me

The Nazarene could hunger and the
    Nazarene could cry
And He could laugh with all the fullness of
    his heart
And those who hardly knew Him
And those who knew Him well
Could feel the contradiction from the start

*C*aesar sought to make himself a god. "I came, I saw, I conquered" was his proud boast. Yet in the time line of history, his kingdom is a mere speck.

Jesus' kingdom was founded on a puzzling twist of Caesar's boast: "I came, I saw, I surrendered." Through the frailty of Jesus' humanity, God the Father displayed His awesome strength. He promises to do the same through the frailty of *our* humanity as well.

26

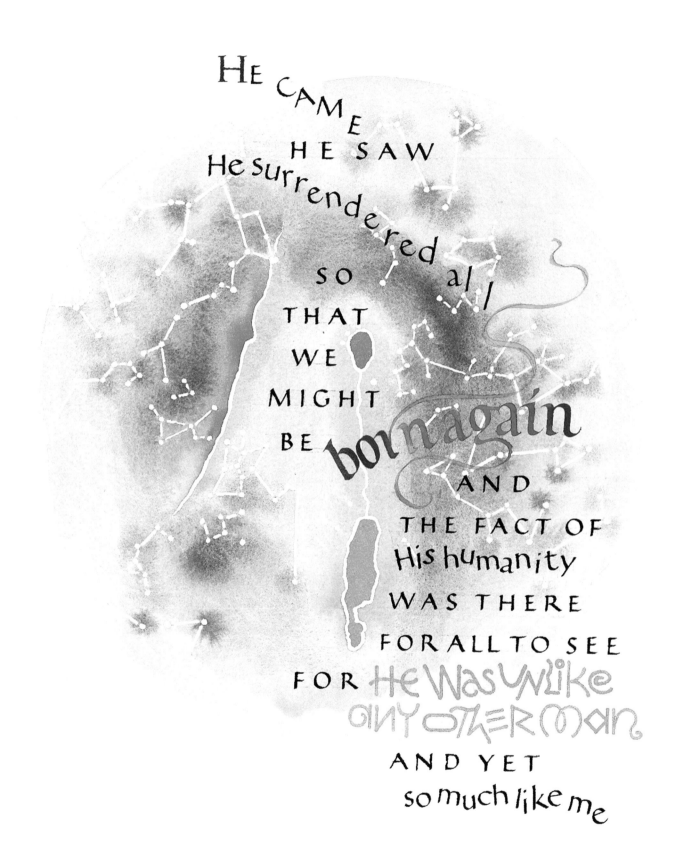

HE CAME
HE SAW
He surrendered all
so
THAT
WE
MIGHT
BE bornagain
AND
THE FACT OF
His humanity
WAS THERE
FOR ALL TO SEE
FOR HE WAS UNLIKE
ANY OTHER MAN
AND YET
so much like me

THE STRANGER

You're still a stranger
Wandering through the wilderness
Still rejected, passed by on the street
Starving, hungry, naked, and cold
Pleading for a cup of cold water
Dying all alone

No longer mistaken
For the rebel You truly are
You would still be tearing up temples
Scattering the money of fools
Scandalizing righteous pretenders
Breaking all the rules

No longer blinded
In the light I see who You really are
Never doing what is expected
Far beyond the frame of my mind
Caring for the poor and neglected
Washing the feet of the beggar on the
    street
While the rich men make believe You'll
    never come

He came to His own, and His own did not receive Him. John 1:11

*I*f we think about it long enough, we might understand why Jesus' contemporaries did not recognize Him. After all, they were misled by their own leaders. And even Jesus Himself didn't always make it easy for them, talking about concepts like eating His flesh without explaining what He meant.

What is more unbelievable is that Jesus remains a stranger to many today—despite the millions of followers who are called by His Name. As He continues to break into the world He alone called into being, His creatures still find nothing familiar. They see only a stranger.

THIS MUST BE THE LAMB

On a gray April morning as a chilling wind
    blew
A thousand dark promises were about to
    come true
As Satan stood trembling, knowing now he
    had lost
As the Lamb took His first step on the way
    to the cross

This must be the Lamb
The fulfillment of all God had spoken
This must be the Lamb
Not a single bone will be broken
Like a sheep to the slaughter
So silently still
This must be the Lamb

They mocked His true calling and laughed
    at His fate
So glad to see the Gentle One consumed by
    their hate
Unaware of the wind and the darkening
    sky
So blind to the fact that it was God limping
    by

The poor women weeping at what seemed
    a great loss
Trembling in fear there at the foot of the
    cross
Tormented by memories that came like a
    flood
Unaware that their pardon must be
    bought by His blood

*I*t was years later that John remembered a detail from the Psalms: Not a single one of His bones would be broken. Perhaps the soldiers could not bring themselves to inflict any more suffering on this "innocent" man. He was already dead.

Did anyone that day see the connection? He had called Himself the Lamb of God. He was gentle and spotless. They slaughtered Him on the cross at precisely the same time they were sacrificing their Passover lambs. Did anyone look into His tender face and think, *This must be the Lamb?*

THIS MUST BE
THE LAMB

The fulfillment of all
God had spoken

Not a single bone will be broken

Like a sheep to the slaughter

SO SILENTLY STILL

CROSS OF GLORY

From the pages of the prophets
He stepped out into the world
And walked the earth in lowly majesty
Though he had been Creator
A creature now was he
Come to bear love's sacred mystery

He the Truth was called a liar
The only lover hated so
He was many times a martyr before he died
Forsaken by the Father
Despised by all the world
He alone was born to be the Crucified

Upon the cross of glory
His death was life to me
A sacrifice of love's most sacred mystery
And death rejoiced to hold him
Though soon he would be free
For love must always have the victory

Though no rhyme could ever tell it
No words could ever say
And no chord is foul enough to sing the
  pain
Still we feel the burden
And suffer with your song
You love us so but yet
You bid us sing

*T*he shame of the cross, a glory? An innocent man dying for a race of thoroughly guilty people? How could it be? Yet this is what we preach and sing and, hopefully, believe. This "foolishness" becomes a pattern for our own lives. Weakness becomes our greatest strength. Dark days turn out to have the most light for our spiritual growth. And ultimately dying to ourselves brings us the only life.

UPON
THE CROSS
OF GLORY
HIS DEATH
WAS LIFE TO ME
A SACRIFICE OF
LOVE'S MOST
SACRED MYSTERY
AND Death rejoiced to hold him
though soon he would be free
FOR Love must
always have
the Victory

LOVE CRUCIFIED AROSE

Long ago He blessed the earth
Born older than the years
And in the stall a cross He saw
Through the first of many tears
A life of homeless wandering
Cast out in sorrow's way
The Shepherd seeking for the lost
His life the price He'd pay

Love crucified arose
The risen One in splendor
Jehovah's soul defender
Has won the victory
Love crucified arose
And the grave became a place of hope

Throughout Your life You felt the weight
Of what You'd come to give
To drink for us that crimson cup
So we might really live
At last the time to love and die
The dark appointed day
That one forsaken moment when
Your Father turned His face away

Love crucified arose
The One who lived and died for me
Was Satan's nail-pierced casualty
Now He's breathing once again
Love crucified arose
And the grave became a place of hope
For the heart that sin and sorrow broke
Is beating once again

*E*mily Dickinson wrote, "When Love was crucified it arose." Somehow that simple line captures the instance of resurrection, before the stone was rolled away. All at once, in the stillness of the tomb, the chest that was motionless starts to rise and fall again. The broken heart is mended by the power of God. Jesus is alive! And so are we.

34

LOVE CRUCIFIED AROSE

The Risen One in splendor
Jehovah's soul defender
has won the victory

AND THE GRAVE BECAME A PLACE OF HOPE
For the heart that sin and sorrow broke
is beating once again
is beating once again

VALLEY OF DRY BONES
(Ezekiel 37:1-10)

Behold a valley filled with bones
Bones on every side
A valley vast, the floor so full
Of bones so very dry

The Lord did ask
Can these bones live?
Might these bones rise once more?
What else was I to say but
You alone can tell oh Lord

A legion now alive
A resurrected army
A living, holy host
Of a people born again

Then prophesy, oh son of man
Cry out to this dead hoard
And when they come to life again
They'll know I am the Lord

And as I spoke what I was told
There came a rattling sound
As bone to bone they formed a mass
Of bodies on the ground

Your dead will come alive
Their graves will lie abandoned
And all those dwelling in the dust
Will wake and shout for joy[1]

And then I called upon the winds
Upon these slain to breathe
At once they stood upon their feet
A mighty, vast army

A legion now alive
A resurrected army
A living, holy host
Of a people born again

Your dead will come alive
Their graves will lie abandoned
And all those dwelling in the dust
Will wake and shout for joy[2]

[1] Isaiah 26:19
[2] Ibid.

The hand of the LORD came upon me and . . . set me down in the midst of the valley; and it was full of bones. Ezekiel 37:1

*O*nce when I climbed one of the hills surrounding the city of Belfast and was standing high above the city, beside a huge war monument, I remembered Ezekiel's vision and the valley of dry bones.

The Irish love that passage. I believe they see, more clearly than I ever could, that this city of theirs, lying in the valley as it does, is the city of Ezekiel's vision. Their experience of the last few hundred years has left them dry, barren, bleached clean. Yet now all over the city a vast army is rising up—not to fight each other but to engage the real enemy, the evil one who has pitted them against themselves for so long. The hand of the Lord has come upon them.

Behold a valley
filled with bones
Bones on every side
A valley vast
the floor so full
of bones so very dry
Your dead will come alive
Their graves will lie abandoned
And all those dwelling in the dust
Will wake and shout for joy

DRAGONSLAYER (The Lamb Triumphant)

The star-led Wizards came to see
Who might this newborn Dragonslayer be[1]
He'd come the serpent's lies to cease
To win for us a never-ending peace

The serpent reared his ugly head in the
    stillness of the garden
To bite the Dragonslayer's heel and defeat
    His plan of pardon[2]
But the Mighty One provided for the fallen
    ones instead[3]
And the quest began to slay the beast, to
    finally crush his head
To finally crush his head

Behold the Dragonslayer
He stills the serpent's scream
He stops his accusations
He spoils the dragon's dream
Behold the Dragonslayer
He died to set us free
The dragon thought he'd won then
It wasn't meant to be
It wasn't meant to be

The dragon sought to take the child of the
    woman clothed in sunlight[4]
But once again the King stepped in and
    began to fight the last fight
And so the battle raged between the
    heavens and the sky
And the dragon was defeated and at last
    was doomed to die
At last was doomed to die

[1] Matthew 2:1-12
[2] Genesis 3:15
[3] Genesis 3:21
[4] Revelation 12:1-5

And war broke out in heaven: Michael and his angels fought with the dragon; and the dragon and his angels fought. Revelation 12:7

Some people were upset that I chose the word *wizard* to describe the Magi (though I actually borrowed it from a poem by Milton). However, it is a good term to describe the wise men. In ancient times men who dealt with astronomy also, by definition, dealt with astrology. They were students of the zodiac and makers of horoscopes. Having worked a lifetime in such dark studies, it is no surprise that they apparently left everything to follow such a bright light.

In a sense they belonged to the dragon up until that time, and now they came to worship the One who would slay the dragon and deliver them from their dark professions. He'd come to still the serpent's lies. To win for all of us a never ending peace.

The
star-led
WIZARDS
came to see
who might
this newborn
DRAGONSLAYER
be
He'd come
the serpent's lies
to cease
to
WIN for us
a neverending
peace

MARANATHA

Maranatha is a cry of the heart
That's hopeful yet weary of waiting
While it may be joyful with the burdens it
  bears
It's sick with anticipating

To long for the Promised One day after day
And the promise that soon He'd return
It's certain that waiting's the most bitter
  lesson
A believing heart has to learn

*Maranatha. How desperate we are just to see
  Your face!*
*Maranatha. To finally fall in Your strong
  embrace!*
A trumpet, a call, and that will be all
*Though it's not yet the hour, the minutes are
  ticking away*

Maranatha is the shout of the few
Who for so long in history've been hiding
Who truly believe that the sound of that
  call
Might actually hasten His coming

For no eye has seen and no ear has yet
  heard
And no mind has ever conceived
The joy of the moment when He will
  appear
To the wonder of all who believe

*He who testifies to these things says, "Surely I
am coming quickly." Amen. Even so, come,
Lord Jesus!* Revelation 22:20

*E*arly in the history of the church the
sound of the word *maranatha* (O Lord,
come!) was thought to hasten the return of
Jesus. The heart cry of His children, many
thought, might influence the Father to
come back sooner. *A naive assumption,* you
might think to yourself.

The same sort of naivete is at the heart
of all prayer. Some call it "childlikeness." I
believe in offering our prayers with the
naive hope that belongs to children. As so
we should shout at the top of our lungs the
special word that might move Him to come
more quickly. *Maranatha!*

FOR NO EYE HAS SEEN
AND NO EAR HAS YET HEARD
AND NO MIND HAS EVER CONCEIVED

the joy of the
moment
WHEN
HE WILL
APPEAR
to the wonder
of all who
believe

Our personal response to the Hound

PART TWO

Those Who Belong to Eternity

of Heaven and our daily journey with Jesus

WILL YOU NOT LISTEN?
(Isaiah 28:23; 51:4)

Is not He who formed the ear
Worth the time it takes to hear?
Should He who formed our lips for
    speaking
Be not heeded when He speaks?

Will you not listen?
Why won't you listen?
God has spoken love to us
Why will you not listen?

Listen to the sacred silence
Listen to the Holy Word
Listen as He speaks through living
Parables that must be heard

Will you not listen?
Why won't you listen?
God has spoken peace to us
Why will you not listen?

He spoke a word of flesh and blood
Flesh and blood that bled and died
Bled and died just to be heard
How could you not hear this Word?
Why will you not hear this Word?

Will you not listen?
Why won't you listen?
God has spoken hope to us

*I*t has been said that we have two ears and only one mouth because God intended us to listen twice as much as we speak.

Our God is a listening God, who does listen twice as much as He speaks. He is a God who cares. He hears our loud cries and tears, our joys and thanksgivings, our disappointments and failures—and still He keeps on listening and caring. Since He has invested so much in listening to us, shouldn't we begin listening more intently to Him—even listening to the silence of Him listening to us?

UNDER THE SUN (Ecclesiastes)

He was a king, a teacher
The wisest in the land
Driven by a passion
Just to know and understand
He opened wide his eyes
Sought to see beyond the lies
And found a world beyond his
    understanding

Under the sun
He saw the vanity of vanities
He bravely looked at life
And saw futility
Torn between the facts he saw
And all he ever had believed
Between his hopes and what he'd clearly
    seen

He hoped it might be wisdom
So he set himself to learn
But found the more the knowledge
The more sorrow and concern
And so he turned to pleasure
To folly and to cheer
But still his laughter
Tasted of his tears

Under the sun
It was all vanity of vanities
In wisdom or in wine
He found futility
In knowledge or in folly
For the wise man or the fool
Hopelessness will always be the rule

And yet there is a time
For everything that's under heaven
A time to run, a time to stand and fight
So in the face of cold despair
No matter what seems right
Remember, darkness drives us to the light

Under the sun
True there is vanity of vanities
But there is more to life
There is security
Remember your Creator
In the days when you are young
And He will be your hope
Under the sun

Remember now your Creator in the days of your youth. Ecclesiastes 12:1

*I*n Ecclesiastes we see the honesty of reason. The result for Solomon—and for us—will always be despair. The wise man, just like the fool, does die. Indeed, things do seem hopeless "under the sun." Yet faith speaks of a hope the intellect cannot grasp.

So at the end of the book the elderly Solomon returns to the simple, trusting faith of his youth. After all his riddles and extravagances, he finally finds what his heart was looking for all along: Someone who transcends words and wisdom. A person he can embrace with his heart.

46

THERE'S A TIME FOR EVERYTHING
UNDER HEAVEN
A TIME TO RUN
A TIME TO STAND AND FIGHT
SO IN THE FACE OF COLD DESPAIR
NO MATTER WHAT SEEMS RIGHT
DARKNESS DRIVES US TO THE LIGHT
TRUE, THERE IS VANITY OF VANITIES
BUT THERE IS MORE TO LIFE
THERE IS SECURITY
REMEMBER YOUR CREATOR
IN THE DAYS WHEN YOU ARE YOUNG
AND HE WILL BE YOUR HOPE
UNDER THE SUN

SEARCH ME AND KNOW ME
(Psalm 139)

Oh my Lord, You search and You know me
You know when I sit, You know when I rise
You know what I think, You know where
   I'm going
Nothing oh Lord, can hide from Your eyes

You close me in, behind and before me
You shield me with Your mighty hand
Such knowledge is too wonderful for me
Too much for me to understand

Where can I go to flee from Your Spirit?
And from Your presence where can I hide?
Behold up in heaven You're there beside
   me
In the depths of the darkness You're by my
   side
And if I rise on the wings of the morning
Or settle on the far side of the sea
Even there Your hand will guide me
For Your right hand is holding me

And if I say the darkness will hide me
The night will shine as bright as day
So search me Lord and lovingly lead me
In Your everlasting Way

You know my sitting down and my rising up.
Psalm 139:2

*D*avid realized that before a thought went through his mind, God already knew it completely. "Such knowledge is too wonderful for me," he admitted.

What seems even more wonderful is that in spite of the fact that God knows us completely, He still *loves us* completely. Despite our dark dimensions, which He knows even better than we do, He is still there—standing at the crest of the hill, arms open wide, waiting with a ring for our foolish finger and shoes for our dirty feet. And when He sees us coming, He runs to meet us, smothering our lame speech of contrition with hugs and kisses.

ABBA FATHER
(Galatians 4:1-7; Romans 8:14-17)

Until your Son called out to me
I was lost
For years my cradle swung above the grave
It is a wondrous thing to be adopted by a
    king
To know a love that crowns and crucifies
And when your spirit moves I breathe a
    prayer to you
I cry not from my mouth but from the heart
Because this spirit came I can use your
    holy name
The tender name a son could only use

Abba Father, Abba Father
Since that word became your covenant name
Abba Father, I cry out to you
Knowing you will hear my plea
For you've adopted me

Your spirit of adoption came and filled my
    heart
To smile upon the earth behind my eyes
Urging me to give, teaching me to live
To show the family likeness of your love
So Jesus has become for me a brother-Lord
The special Son who died to set us free
His cross for me has won the right to be
    your son
A blessed son You'll never cast aside

For you did not receive the spirit of bondage
again to fear, but you received the Spirit of
adoption by whom we cry out, "Abba,
Father." Romans 8:15

*T*hose who say Jesus was the first to call God "Father" do not have their facts quite right. Many other groups, including the Pharisees, referred to God as "Father." Jesus was borrowing from one of their prayer formulas when He prayed, "Our Father in heaven ..."

But what was completely unheard of was the reference to God as "Abba"—an Aramaic word which is essentially baby talk. In Hebrew *ab* means father; hence *Ab*-raham means "father of a multitude." When a baby first tries to say *ab* it invariably comes out as "abba." And this is the word Jesus used.

Sloppy sentimentality? Arrogant assumption? Or, rather, was it the heart cry of One who saw even Himself as little in God's eyes, as God's little boy? Abba Father becomes the call of all who have been adopted into God's wonderful family of faith. He is our Papa!

IT IS A WONDROUS THING

abba
father

i cry out to you
knowing
you will hear my plea.
for you've adopted
me

TO BE ADOPTED BY A KING

I WILL BRING YOU HOME
(Zephaniah 3:20)

Though you are homeless
Though you're alone
I will be your Home
Whatever's the matter
Whatever's been done
I will be your Home

I will be your Home
I will be your Home
In this fearful, fallen place
I will be your Home

When time reaches fullness
When I move My hand
I will bring you home
Home to your own place
In a beautiful land
I will bring you home

I will bring you home
I will bring you home

From this fearful, fallen place
I will bring you home
I will bring you home

*O*ur longing for home is one proof that
we were created in God's image, for our
God is a God of the home. In the Old
Testament God promises His stubborn
people a home—the promised land—and
all but drives them towards it. In the New
Testament He offers the hope of heaven as
a home. "In my Father's house there are
many places to stay," Jesus promises. The
Lord of Creation desires one day to share
that home with us.

52

Though you are homeless
Though you're alone
whatever's the matter
whatever's been done
In this fearful
fallen place
I will be
your home

JUBILEE (Leviticus 25)

The Lord provided for a time
For the slaves to be set free
For the debts to all be cancelled
So His chosen ones could see

His deep desire was for forgiveness
He longed to see their liberty
And His yearning was embodied
In the Year of Jubilee

Jubilee, Jubilee
Jesus is our Jubilee
Debts forgiven
Slaves set free
Jesus is our Jubilee

At the Lord's appointed time
His deep desire became a man
The heart of all true jubilation
And with joy we understand
In His voice we hear a trumpet sound
That tells us we are free
He is the incarnation
Of the year of Jubilee

To be so completely guilty
Given over to despair
To look into your judge's face
And see a Savior there

That fiftieth year shall be a Jubilee to you; in it you shall neither sow nor reap what grows of its own accord, nor gather the grapes of your untended vine. Leviticus 25:11

*J*esus told the people they were slaves, but they would not believe him. "We have never been slaves to anyone!" they retorted. But Jesus pointed out to them: "You are in slavery to sin, the worst slavery of all."

In the Old Testament God spoke a wonderful word to slaves. Every fifty years all debts were cancelled, and they were set free! *Freedom*, the one word every slave longs to hear. In the New Testament God spoke another Word, His final Word. It too is a word of freedom, a jubilee. That Word was spoken in syllables of flesh and blood. *Jesus.*

To be so completely guilty
Given over to despair
To look into your judge's face
And see a Savior there

JUBILEE
JUBILEE
JESUS
IS OUR
JUBILEE

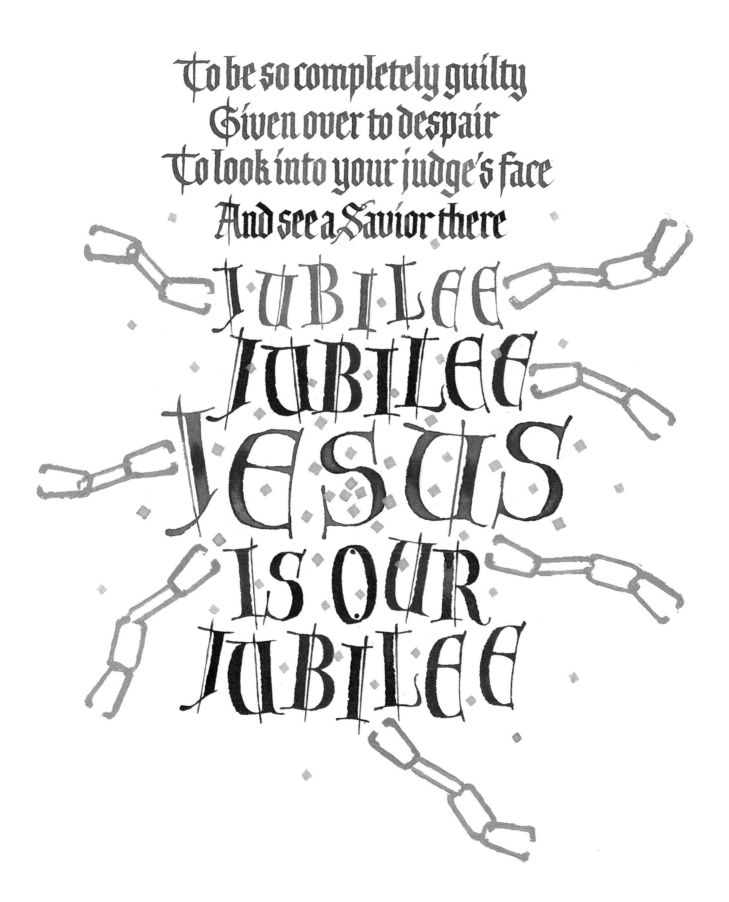

JESUS LOVES ME

Jesus loves me, this I know
It's not just the Bible that tells me so
I can feel it, feel it in my soul
Jesus loves me, this I know

Jesus loves me, I know it's true
Because He died for me, and He died for
    you
When I think of all the pain that He went
    through
I want the world to know and I want to
    shout the news

Jesus loves me, how can it be?
That the only Son of God should care
    about me
To wash away my sin and set me free
To take my life and make it all it's meant to
    be

Jesus loves me, and He loves you too
You can't understand it all, just believe it's
    true
And He'll take away your old heart and
    give you one that's new
You'll feel the walls come down as His love
    comes shining through

*T*his is an adaptation of the very first song most of us learn. And that is as it should be because the words contain a lesson most of us will spend the rest of our lives learning: *Jesus loves me.* This is the foundation for all that has meaning in life.

The second part—*For the Bible tells me so*—is just as important. The Word of God is the source, and without it we would be left to guess at who Jesus is and what He means. I met people in China who made such guesses. They looked at creation and reasoned their way to a loving God. Not until they read a Bible, though, did they learn the name and heart of Jesus.

THE POEM OF YOUR LIFE
(Ephesians 2:10)

Life is a song
We must sing with our days
A poem with meaning
More than words can say
A painting with colors
No rainbow can tell
A lyric that rhymes
Either heaven or hell

We are living letters
That doubt desecrates
We're the notes of the song
Of the chorus of faith
God shapes every second
Of our little lives
And minds every minute
As the universe waits by

The pain and the longing
The joy and the moments of light
Are the rhythm and rhyme
The free verse of the
Poem of life

So look in the mirror
And pray for the grace
To tear off the mask
See the art of your face
Open your earlids
And hear the sweet song
Of each moment that passes
And pray to prolong

Your time in the ball
Of the dance of your days
Your canvas of colors
Of moments ablaze
With all that is holy
With the joy and the strife
With the rhythm and rhyme
Of the poem of your life
With the rhythm and rhyme
Of the poem of your life

For we are His workmanship, created in Christ Jesus for good works, which God prepared beforehand that we should walk in them. Ephesians 2:10

*W*e are God's "poiema"—His handiwork, His artful creation, His poems. The same One who speaks most directly, clearly, and authoritatively through His Word also speaks through the silence of prayer and the everydayness of our lives. The events, the people who move in and out of our lives, are verses of the song He is singing through us.

If all this is true, and I believe it is, then nothing else matters but listening. To His Word. To the silence. To the poem of our lives.

LOOK IN THE MIRROR
AND PRAY FOR THE GRACE
TO TEAR OFF THE MASK
SEE THE ART OF YOUR FACE
OPEN YOUR EARLIDS
AND HEAR THE SWEET SONG
OF EACH MOMENT THAT PASSES

AND PRAY TO PROLONG
YOUR TIME IN THE BALL
OF THE DANCE OF YOUR DAYS
YOUR CANVAS OF COLORS
OF MOMENTS ABLAZE
WITH ALL THAT IS HOLY
WITH THE JOY AND THE STRIFE
OF THE RHYTHM AND RHYME
OF THE POEM OF YOUR LIFE

FACE THE LIGHT

Face the Light, don't stumble in the
    darkness
Face the Light, see how dark your heart is
Face the Light, you'll never see the shadows
Only face the Light

Face the Light, don't know how much you
    need Him
Face the Light, just turn around and see
    Him
Face the Light, He'll take away the shadows
Only face the Light

There's a force in the dark that's waiting
    for you
And it's telling your heart what it wants to
    do
But the Light is there and it wants to shine
    through
You'll never know how dark you are inside
    till you face the Light

There are just two ways, and you'd better
    choose right
You can die in the dark, or you can live in
    the Light
One is the Way, the Truth, the Life
The other's dark and never leads to home

*N*o shadows, no gray. Just the black, black night. The line between darkness and light is as clearly drawn as the line that divides night from day. We can try to walk in the dark, Jesus says. But we will stumble and fall because we were meant to be creatures of the light. Created for the light, by the Light.

Though the world will try to convince us that shadows are all we were meant for, the Word of God tells us we can choose the light. It's where we belong.

HOW LONG? (Psalm 13)

How long will you forget, oh Lord?
How long, how long?
How I long to see your face, oh Lord
How long will you hide?
How I struggle with my thoughts, oh Lord
How long, how long?
Suffer sorrow in my heart, oh Lord
How long will you hide?

How long?
How long?

Look on me and give an answer Lord
How long, how long?
Give me light or I can live no more
How long will you hide?
My foes rejoice when they see me fall
How long, how long?
"We have overcome him now," they call
How long will you hide?

How long?

Still, oh Lord, you are so good to me
How long, how long?
My heart rejoices how you set me free
How long will you hide?
Lord, I sing for what I'm hoping of
How long, how long?
How I trust in your unfailing love
How long will you hide?

How long?

How long, O LORD? Will You forget me forever?
How long will You hide Your face from me?
Psalm 13:1

Many times we join the faithless-sounding choruses of the faithful who have cried out through the centuries, "How long, how long, O Lord? How long?"

But for God's grace, our burden would be unbearable. But for His love, our life unlivable. But for the hope of someday seeing His beautiful, holy face and hearing "Well done," there would be no point or purpose.

So, Lord … How long? How long?

TRAITOR'S LOOK

How did it feel to take the place
Of honor at the meal
To take the sop from His own hands
A prophesy to seal
Was it because He washed your feet
That you sold Him as a slave?
The Son of Man, the Lamb of God
Who'd only come to save

The silver that they paid to you
From out of their precious till
Was meant to buy a spotless lamb
A sacrifice to kill
How heavy was the money bag
That couldn't set you free
It became a heavy millstone
As you fell into the sea

Now Judas don't you come too close
I fear that I might see
The traitor's look upon your face
Might look too much like me
'Cause just like you I've sold the Lord
And often for much less
And like a wretched traitor
I betrayed Him with a kiss

*J*udas could have simply pointed to Jesus and said, "That's him over there." His kiss was unnecessary. So why betray Jesus with a kiss?

I have heard that we all betray the Lord with a kiss. Once we have given our lives to Him, every sin we willingly commit is a similar betrayal. If that is true, then we are all Judases. And we are all Peters as well, denying that we know Him by our arrogant attitudes.

Yet these two men reacted differently after their sin. And so can we. We can despair and hang, like Judas, not believing in the Lord's gracious forgiveness. Or like Peter, we can jump in the water and swim to Him on the shore—trusting in His forgiving love.

Now
JUDAS
Don't you come
too close
I fear that i might see
the traitor's look
upon your face
might look too much
like me

JOY IN THE JOURNEY

There is a joy in the journey
There's a light we can love on the way
There is a wonder and wildness to life
And freedom for those who obey

And all those who seek it
Shall find it[1]
A pardon for all who believe
A hope for the hopeless
And sight for the blind[2]

To all who've been born of the Spirit
And who share incarnation with Him
Who belong to eternity
Stranded in time
And weary of struggling with sin

Forget not the hope
That's before you
And never stop counting the cost
Remember the hopelessness
When you were lost?

[1] Proverbs 8:17
[2] Isaiah 42:7

*O*ur youngest daughter, Maggie, took her first real steps today. The look on her face was impossible to describe. *This is it!* I thought. *The first steps of a lifetime, the beginning of her journey.* And on that little face I saw pure joy, despite her fear of falling. The reason? Her mother was behind her, and her father was in front of her, ready to catch her if she fell.

We are all fallen and falling. Yet our Father is always there, encouraging us to take the next step. So shouldn't there be joy on our faces and in our hearts, despite our fear of falling?

There is a joy in the journey
THERE'S A LIGHT WE CAN LOVE ON THE WAY
There is a wonder and wildness to life
AND FREEDOM FOR THOSE WHO OBEY

THINGS WE LEAVE BEHIND

There sits Simon so foolishly wise
Proudly he's tending his nets
Then Jesus calls and the boats drift away
And all that he owns he forgets
But more than the nets he abandoned
    that day
He found that his pride was soon drifting
    away
And it's hard to imagine the freedom we
    find
From the things we leave behind[1]

Matthew was mindful of taking the tax
And pressing the people to pay
But hearing the call he responded in faith
And followed the Light and the Way
And leaving the people so puzzled he
    found
The greed in his heart was no longer
    around
And it's hard to imagine the freedom we
    find
From the things we leave behind[2]

Every heart needs to be set free
From possessions that hold it so tight
'Cause freedom's not found in the things
    that we own
It's the power to do what is right
With Jesus, our only possession
Then giving becomes our delight
And we can't imagine the freedom we find
From the things we leave behind

We show a love for the world in our lives
By worshipping goods we possess
When Jesus says, "Lay all your treasures
    aside
And love God above all the rest"
'Cause when we say no to the things of the
    world
We open our hearts to the love of the Lord
And it's hard to imagine the freedom we
    find
From the things we leave behind

[1] Matthew 4:18
[2] Mark 2:13

*T*his song was born from a sermon. Years ago William Lane showed my wife, Susan, and I that almost everyone who followed Jesus in the New Testament left something behind. The woman at the well, her bucket. The blind beggar, the cloak he used to catch coins. Matthew, his tax table. Peter, his boats and nets. John, his poor old father, Zebedee.

Possessions are not so much things we own as they are things that own a little bit of us. We all need to ask ourselves, "What have I left behind to follow Him?"

every heart
needs to be free
from
possessions
that hold it
so tight

because

freedom's
not found
in the
things
that we own

it's the
power to do
what is
right

with Jesus
our only
possession

then

It's hard
to imagine
the freedom
we find

from the things
we leave
behind

giving
becomes
our delight

GOD'S OWN FOOL

It seems I've imagined him all of my life
As the wisest of all of mankind
But if God's holy wisdom is foolish to men
He must have seemed out of His mind
For even His family said He was mad[1]
And the priests said a demon's to blame[2]
For God in the form of this angry young
    man
Could not have seemed perfectly sane

When we in our foolishness thought we were
    wise
He played the fool and He opened our eyes
When we in our weakness believed we were
    strong
He became helpless to show we were wrong
And so we follow God's own fool
For only the foolish can tell
Believe the unbelievable
And come be a fool as well

So come lose your life for a carpenter's son
For a madman who died for a dream
Then you'll have the faith His first
    followers had
And you'll feel the weight of the beam
So surrender the hunger to say you must
    know
Have the courage to say "I believe"
For the power of paradox opens your eyes
And blinds those who say they can see

[1] Mark 3:21
[2] Mark 3:22

For the message of the cross is foolishness to those who are perishing, but to us who are being saved it is the power of God.
1 Corinthians 1:18

*I*n the end, explains Paul, Christ's foolishness and ours reveal the deep, hidden wisdom of God. And His weakness and ours expose the impotence of all the things the world considers to be powerful. Paul called it the "foolishness" of what we believe. The Son of God died for sinners, like you and me. This utterly unbelievable good news, says author and theologian Frederich Buechner, "is not too good to be true, but rather too good not to be true"!

When
We in our foolishness
thought we were wise
He played the fool and
he opened our eyes
When we in our weakness
believed we were strong
He became helpless
to show we were wrong
and so we follow
God's own fool
for only the foolish can tell
Believe the unbelievable
and come be a fool as well

CHORUS OF FAITH

Sing it with your life, sing with your heart
Make melody with the words of your mouth
But mind that you listen, tell it to others
Hear the chorus of faith
Live the chorus of faith

The first note of the song split the darkness
And was sung by the planets and stars
And their light spoke "hallelujah"
And the words of the chorus
Were sung by angels before us
Now come join in the tune

Then in time Jesus came to be for us
And His Coming made our life a song
And His Word is the chorus
Is the Light that is burning
Is the Truth beyond learning
Is the reason we sing

Singing this song's what life is about
And if you refuse the stones will cry out
We do not sing that we might be more
   blessed
He loves us with passion, without regret
He cannot love more and will not love less

*A*ll around us we hear the music of creation: the singing of birds, the symphonies of color and form, the hallelujah of all God has made. His Spirit places a song in our hearts too—a song we are meant to sing every day with all that is in us. The song of faith. Only through this grace can we praise God with all the saints. May the sound of the song of our lives make His heart glad!

Our relationship to family and

PART THREE

The Call Is to Community

the ever-expanding ranks of God's people

ARISE, MY LOVE (Song of Solomon)

Arise, my love, my lovely one come
The winter is past and the rains are gone
The flowers appear, it's the season of song
My beautiful one, arise and come with me

Who is it that appears like the dawn?
As fair as the moon, as bright as the sun
Show me your face, let me hear your voice
My beautiful one, arise and come with me

Set me like a seal on your heart
For love is unyielding as the grave
The flash of it is a jealous fire
No flood can quench
For love is as strong as death

Arise, my love and come with me
Before the dawn breaks and the shadows
     flee
You ravished my heart with just one glance
My beautiful one, arise and come with me

Do not arouse or awaken love
Until it so desires

Arise, my love, my lovely one come
The winter is past and the rains are gone
The flowers appear, it's the season of song
My beautiful one, arise and come with me
I am my love's, my beloved's mine
Arise and come with me

By night on my bed I sought the one I love.
Song of Solomon 3:1

Solomon, so famous for his wisdom, also possessed a most remarkably romantic soul. We see this in his song, "Canticum Canticorum" in old Latin, or Song of Songs.

These days we view people "in love" with a sort of pitiful compassion. "They have lost their minds," we say, with a sad twinkle in our eyes. Yet this is not the love we read about in Solomon's song. Here is a passion we can scarcely understand. Powerful and fierce, and wise in a way that only love can be wise.

I AM MY LOVE'S AND MY BELOVED IS MINE

THE WINTER IS PAST
and the rains are gone
The flowers appear
It's the season of song
my beautiful one
arise and come with me

THE WEDDING (John 2)

Lord of Light
Oh come to this wedding
Take the doubt and darkness away
Turn the water of lifeless living
To the wine of gladness we pray

Mother Mary's gently requesting
That You might do whatever You can
Though she may be impatient
She loves You
And so she asks what she can't understand

So amidst the laughter and feasting
There sits Jesus full with the fun
He has made them wine
Because He is longing
For a wedding that's yet to come

Now both Jesus and His disciples were invited
to the wedding. John 2:2

A doubt and a darkness lurk behind
even our most celebrative moments. Most
who weep at a wedding weep for joy. Yet
some—particularly moms and dads—cry
because they know how painful a life
together can be.

That is why we invite Jesus to our
weddings. The formal service refers to the
holy estate, which He "adorned and
beautified with His presence." Simply by
being there He drives the darkness away.

LORD OF LIGHT

O COME TO
THIS WEDDING
TAKE THE DOUBT
AND DARKNESS AWAY
TURN THE WATER
OF LIFELESS LIVING
TO THE WINE
OF GLADNESS

HOME

Home is a comfort
And home is a light
A place to leave the darkness outside
Home is a peaceful and ever-full feeling
A place where a soul safely hides

And being at home
Should remind you that still
There's a place that's prepared
Just for you
And I think my home
Is just heaven's reflection
As long as my home's here with you

Home is where someone is waiting and
    loving
And happy to see you again
That half of your heart
That somebody else treasures
The one who's your forever friend

But it seems that He's told me
The life that He's showing me
Is a life mostly spent on the road
And when the world's empty charm
Has done all of its harm
I know that His love waits for me in your
    arms

*J*esus' description of heaven in the Bible is characteristically sparse. He described it as a place where He was going to make preparations just for us. This reminds us of His servanthood in our lives. Jesus is preparing a place just for us, right now.

One word best describes what such a place will be: *home.* Until we finally go to be with Him—or He comes to get us—we will no doubt suffer a kind of heavenly homesickness.

HOME

IS A COMFORT
and home is a light
a place to leave the darkness outside
Home is a peaceful and
ever-full feeling
a place where a soul safely hides
and being at home
should remind you that still
there's a place that's prepared

just for you

COME TO THE CRADLE

Come to the cradle
Come and find peace
Alone in the cradle
Simplicity sleeps
Behold, perfect wisdom
So gentle and mild
In the innocent, upward
Trusting glance of a child

Come hear the call
Of sweet sighs
In the dark
Their touch is tender
It touches your heart
The bustle and business
Lasts year after year
But this little baby
Won't always be here

When God gives a gift
He wraps it up in a child
He made them
Loves them
So wondrously wild
And so you are chosen
And called out for prayer
So come to the cradle
He waits for you there

I know of no place where more prayer occurs than beside a crib. There we give thanks. There we wrestle with the future on our infant's behalf. There we fight off the minions of the world that await the child.

A contrast exists in the nursery. The adult agonizes in prayer; the infant sleeps. Together they sing a song of experience and wisdom. The hard-earned experience of the worrying adult; the wisdom of the innocent baby.

COME TO THE CRADLE
COME AND FIND PEACE
ALONE IN THE CRADLE
SIMPLICITY SLEEPS
BEHOLD, PERFECT WISDOM
SO GENTLE AND MILD
IN THE INNOCENT, UPWARD
TRUSTING GLANCE OF A CHILD
WHEN GOD
GIVES A GIFT
HE WRAPS IT
UP IN A CHILD

BUSY HANDS, BUSY FEET

Busy hands
Busy feet
Busy mind
Go to sleep
Now let go
Of your fight
Say hello
To the night

Close your eyes
Go to bed
Give it up
Sleepyhead
Teary eyes
Shaky chin
It's a fight
You can't win

Don't you worry
Don't you fret
In your sleep
You'll forget
That the work
Of the day
Is the business
Of play

*L*ast night our two-year-old, Nathan, who is usually somewhat of a loner, climbed into my lap and fell asleep in thirty seconds, as if he had pulled over to the side of the road and called it a night. When it is time to sleep, nothing can stop him. When it is time to play, he does so with all that is in him.

His busyness somehow seems more redemptive than mine. When I am working, a part of me is somewhere else. And I usually fall asleep only after a hard-fought battle with an endless list of worries. Perhaps the way Nate plays is the way I should learn to work.

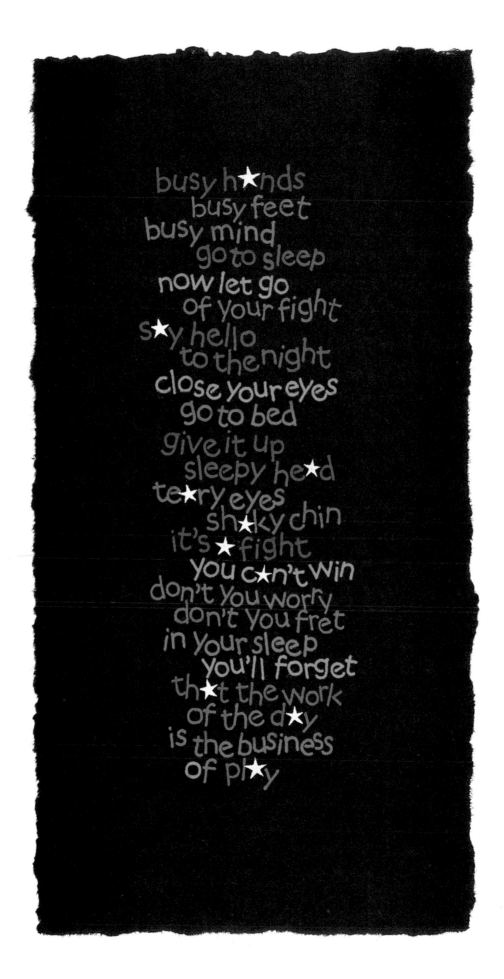

A SONG FOR THE NIGHT

Like a warm woolen blanket
The dark wraps around
As we cuddle together
And hear all the sounds
Of the night as it's falling
And coming to be
Now look with your ears
Not your eyes, and you'll see

Good night to the trees
So majestic and strong
Good night to the birds
With their wonderful songs
Good night to the planets
That wander above
Good night to a universe
Alive with Your love

The sounds of the night
Are the notes of a song
So secret and sacred
So beautifully strong
In the air there's an echo
A whisper and a prayer
And though He's not seen
Still the Singer is there

So good night to creation
To the bright shining stars
Good night to the moon
Faithful witness you are
Good night to the world
As it hurtles through space
Good night to the wonder
In your shining face

With all that is waiting
The sights and the sounds
Your wondrous world
Like a merry-go-round
Is it any wonder
It's so hard to sleep
While outside You're playing
Your own hide-and-seek

S leep does not come easy to most babies. Until I became a father I never thought to ask, "Why all the struggle to avoid something that is such a relief?"

Then I experienced the world through their eyes. Everything is new, every sight fresh, every sound formerly unheard. There is no drudgery. To surrender to sleep and leave this wonderful world is unthinkable.

As we sing them to sleep my wife and I sometimes wonder if we should be more like our children. Perhaps we should fight for the chance to experience just one more of His miracles before we surrender to sleep.

GOODNIGHT
to the trees *trees*
trees GOODNIGHT *trees*
trees so majestic and strong

GOODNIGHT
birds to the birds *birds* *birds*
with their wonderful songs

GOODNIGHT
THE PLANETS S
TO THE PLANETS
THAT WANDER ABOVE

GOODNIGHT
to a universe
alive with your love

COME TO THE TABLE

Come to the table
And savor the sight
The wine and the bread that was broken
And all have been welcome to come
If they might
Accept as their own these two tokens
The bread is His body
The wine is the blood
And the one who provides them is true
He freely offers
We freely receive
To accept and believe Him is all we must do

Come to the table
And taste of the glory
And savor the sorrow
He's dying tomorrow
The hand that is breaking the bread
Soon will be broken
And here at the table
Sit those who have loved Him
One is a traitor and one will deny
Though He's lived His life for them all
And for all be crucified

Come to the table He's prepared for you
The bread of forgiveness, the wine of
    release
Come to the table and sit down beside Him
The Savior wants you to join in the feast

Come to the table and see in His eyes
The love that the Father has spoken
And know you are welcome
Whatever your crime
Though every commandment you've
    broken
For He's come to love you
And not to condemn
And He offers a pardon of peace
If you'll come to the table
You'll feel in your heart
The greatest forgiveness
The greatest release

And He sent Peter and John, saying, "Go and prepare the Passover for us, that we may eat." Luke 22:8

*W*e are not ready to come to the table of the Lord until we realize how completely unworthy we are to be there. That is why Paul instructs us to examine ourselves in 1 Corinthians, chapter 11.

I once heard a sermon that helped me better understand all this. Just when I was ready to run out of the church because of the weight of my sin and unworthiness, the pastor issued an invitation to the banquet of Life. He said, "If you are that kind of guilty person, then this table is for you."

I hear those words every time I come to the table of Jesus. And each time I feel like rushing to the table to receive the priceless gift that has been so graciously offered to me.

Come to the table
He's prepared just for you
The bread of forgiveness
the wine of release
Come to the table
and sit down beside Him
The Savior wants you
to join in the feast
Come to the table
and see in His eyes
The love that the Father
has spoken
And know you are welcome
Whatever your crime
Though every commandment
you've broken
For He's come to love you
And not to condemn
And He offers a pardon
of peace

THE BASIN AND THE TOWEL

In an upstairs room
A parable is just about to come alive
And while they bicker about who's best
With a painful glance He'll silently rise
Their Savior Servant must show them how
Through the will of the water
And the tenderness of the towel

And the call is to community
The impoverished power that sets the soul free
In humility to take the vow
That day after day we must take up
The basin and towel

In any ordinary place
On any ordinary day
The parable can live again
When one will kneel and one will yield
Our Savior Servant must show us how
Through the will of the water
And the tenderness of the towel

And the space between ourselves
     sometimes
Is more than the distance between the stars
By the fragile bridge of the servant's bow
We take up the basin and the towel

After that, He poured water into a basin and begun to wash the disciples' feet, and to wipe them with the towel with which He was girded. John 13:5

*T*his song is about a moment when Jesus gave up on words. In the face of an ongoing argument about which disciple would be the greatest, Jesus silently got up from the table and washed their feet.

He had always been their servant, as much their butler as their Master. He fed them and risked His life to defend them. And now, on their last night together He dressed Himself like a slave and lived out His favorite role: that of a servant. If we do not know Jesus as the Servant Lord, we do not really know Him. This is the shape of His life, the desire of His heart, and the pattern He has laid down for us to follow. We are to take up the basin and the towel.

THE CALL IS TO

COMMUNITY

THE IMPOVERISHED POWER

THAT SETS THE SOUL FREE

IN HUMILITY · TO TAKE THE VOW

THAT DAY AFTER DAY

WE MUST TAKE UP THE BASIN AND THE TOWEL

IN ANY ORDINARY PLACE

ON ANY ORDINARY DAY

THE PARABLE CAN *L*IVE AGAIN

WHEN ONE WILL KNEEL

AND ONE WILL YIELD

OUR SAVIOR / SERVANT

MUST SHOW US HOW

THROUGH THE WILL OF THE WATER

AND THE TENDERNESS OF THE TOWEL

SO MANY BOOKS, SO LITTLE TIME
(Amos 8:11)

There is a hunger, a longing for bread
And so comes the call for the poor to be fed
More hungry by far are a billion and more
Who wait for the Bread of the Word of the
    Lord

So many books, so little time
So many hunger, so many blind
Starving for words, they must wait in the night
To open a Bible and move towards the Light

There'll come a time, the prophets
    would say
When the joy of mankind will be withered
    away[1]
A want not for water, but a hunger for
    more
A famine for hearing the Word of the Lord[2]

The Word won't go out
Except it return
Full, overflowing[3]
And so we must learn

[1] Joel 1:12
[2] Amos 8:11
[3] Isaiah 55:11

92

"Behold, the days are coming," says the Lord
GOD, "That I will send a famine on the land,
not a famine of bread, nor a thirst for water,
but of hearing the words of the LORD."
Amos 8:11

Years ago a friend gave me a T-shirt with the name of his bookstore on the front and a motto on the back: "So many books, so little time." When I went to China to help smuggle Bibles, I decided to wear this shirt as a subtle witness. Alone in the hotel room the night after we had accomplished our mission, the shirt lay across the bed. All at once those words took on a whole new meaning. They became a song.

Amos said that there would be a famine in the last days, even though food and water were abundant. People would be starving for something more important. This prophecy is being fulfilled in China where billions are starving for the Word of God. Behold, the days have come!

There is a hunger
SO MANY BOOKS
a longing for Bread
SO LITTLE TIME
And so comes the call
SO MANY HUNGER
for the poor to be fed
SO MANY BLIND
More hungry by far
STARVING FOR WORDS
are a billion and more
THEY MUST WAIT IN THE NIGHT
who wait for the Bread
TO OPEN A BIBLE
of the Word of the Lord
AND MOVE TOWARDS THE LIGHT

THE GREENING OF BELFAST

In a green, green land, riding on the sea
Live a people who speak like a song
But their fertile field lies so fallow and bare
And has borne bitter fruit for so long

Pray for the greening of Belfast
That what is now barren
Might bloom and be fair
God loves the city of Belfast
For so many children who love Him live there
So many children who love Him live there

The verdant hills like strong arms embrace
A heartbreaking, heartbroken town
With the air so full of angels there
It's not hard to imagine the sound
Of their cries and tears
Of their pleas and prayers
For their city to know peace once more
Let the fighting cease
Let the saints be released
To join in true spiritual war

*U*ntil you've seen the green fields of the Emerald Isle, you can't really know what "greenness" is. Words like *verdant* or *lush* fall to the ground. The paradox is how such a green land could at the same time be so barren and so torn apart by struggle.

Yet hope has not died in Ireland; it has just slept beneath a long winter. Prayer has preserved the green grass of freedom from the drought of fear. And prayer has begun a great thaw in the land and in people's hearts. By God's grace, the spring has come.

In a green, green land
riding on the sea
live a people
who speak like a song

But their fertile field
lies so fallow and bare
and has borne bitter fruit
for so long

Pray for the greening
of Belfast
that what is now barren
might bloom and be fair

God loves the
city of Belfast
for so many children
who love him live there

HEAL OUR LAND
(Song for the National Day of Prayer)

Forgive oh Lord
And heal our land
And give us eyes to seek Your face
And hearts to understand

That You alone
Make all things new
And the blessings of the land we love
Are really gifts from You

If My people will humbly pray
And seek My face and turn away
From all their wicked ways
Then I will hear them and move My hand
And freely then will I forgive
And I will heal their land

Unite our hearts (unite our hearts)
In one accord (in one accord)
And make us hungry for Your peace
And burdened for the poor

And grant us hope (and grant us hope)
That we might see (that we might see)
The future for the land we love
Our life, our liberty

If My people who are called by My name will humble themselves, and pray and seek My face, and turn from their wicked ways, then I will hear from heaven, and will forgive their sin and heal their land. 2 Chronicles 7:14

*I*t doesn't take a political analyst or historian to tell us our country is sick. As we have gradually departed from the rich biblical heritage of our forefathers, we have become, year after year, day after day, weaker and more sickly.

The Word of God provides the only cure: prayer. In the face of the open wound that is America—a hopeless quagmire of immorality and greed—prayer promises the only hope and healing.

If my people

Then I will hear them

will humbly pray

and move my hand

And seek my face

And freely then

and turn away

will I forgive

from all their wicked ways

And I will heal their land

THE LAMB IS A LION

Weak from the journey
The long traveling days
Hungry to worship
To join in the praise
Shock met with anger
That burned on His face
As He entered the wasteland
Of that barren place

And the Lamb is a Lion
Who's roaring with rage
At the empty religion
That's filling their days
They'll flee from the harm
Of the Carpenter's strong arm
And come to know the scourging
Anger of the Lord

The priests and the merchants
Demanded some proof
For their hearts were hardened
And blind to the truth
That Satan's own law
Is to sell and to buy
But God's only Way
Is to give and to die

But one of the elders said to me, "Do not weep. Behold, the Lion of the tribe of Judah, the Root of David, has prevailed to open the scroll and to loose its seven seals." And I looked, and behold, in the midst of the throne and of the four living creatures, and in the midst of the elders, stood a Lamb as though it had been slain, having seven horns and seven eyes, which are the seven Spirits of God sent out into all the earth. Revelation 5:5-6

*J*onathan Edwards said that the power of the gospel comes from the irreconcilable images of Jesus, which nonetheless make perfect sense to the mind of faith. He is both God and man, an impossible combination. The Shepherd and the Lamb. The Lamb and the Lion.

This last great image is resolved in Revelation as John stands weeping because the scroll cannot be opened. One of the elders says to John, "Behold, the Lion has prevailed." John expects to see a lion; instead, a wounded lamb appears in the midst of the elders.

"Our Lamb has conquered, Him let us follow" was the creed of the ancient church. An impossible creed. And that's precisely why it is so awesomely powerful.

The Lamb

IS A

Lion

who's roaring with rage

at the empty Religion

that's filling their days

for their hearts were hardened

and blind to the Truth

that Satan's own law is to sell and to buy

BUT GOD'S ONLY WAY

is to give and to die

LULLABY FOR THE INNOCENTS

Hear now a lullaby
You'll never hear
For your life was something
That wasn't held dear
You need not a lullaby
For you do not weep
Nor love's arms to hold you
In death you do sleep

What your life might have been
We'll never know
A miracle happened
But there's nothing to show
We're left with this sorrow
But hope all the same
That in heaven there's Someone
Who knows you by name

This song is never supposed to be sung. There is, in fact, no music. It needs none for it will never be heard by the millions of infants who will never be sung to sleep, never be cradled in the tenderness of a mother's arms, and never hear the soothing sound of a father's voice.

You might respond to that thought, "Grim emotional manipulation. Sentimentalism." Perhaps, but the facts are certain—as certain as the fact that this song will never be sung.

What your life might have been
we'll never know
A miracle happened
But there's nothing
to show
We're left with
this sorrow
But hope all the same
That in heaven
there's Someone
who knows you by name

DISTRESSING DISGUISE

He is in the pain, He is in the need
He is in the poor, we are told to feed
Though He was rich for us, He became
    poor
How could He give so much? What was it
    for?

In His distressing disguise
He waits for us to surmise
That we rob our brothers by all that we
    own
And that's not the way He has shown

Every time a faithful servant serves a
    brother that's in need
What happens at that moment is a miracle
    indeed
As they look to one another in an instant it
    is clear
Only Jesus is visible for they've both
    disappeared

He is in the hand that reaches out to give
He is in the touch that causes us to live
So speak with your life now as well as your
    tongue
Shelter the homeless and care for the
    young

In His distressing disguise
He hopes that we'll realize
That when we take care of the poorest of
    them
We've really done it to him[1]

[1] Matthew 26:11

"And the King will answer and say to them, 'Assuredly, I say to you, inasmuch as you did it to one of the least of these My brethren, you did it to Me.'" Matthew 25:40

Jesus' radical identification with the poor and dispossessed set Him apart in His age. Certainly religious people practiced acts of charity. Giving to the poor was a righteous work, as important as studying the Torah, the rabbis taught.

Giving money was one thing. But Jesus gave Himself to the poor. He opened not just His purse but the door of His life to them. When we follow His example, we will discover that Jesus Himself enters our lives. In feeding the hungry we ourselves will find a feast.

He is in the pain,
He is in the need
He is in the poor,
we are told to feed
He is in the hand
that reaches out to give
He is in the touch
that causes us to live
So speak with your life now
as well as your tongue

Shelter the
homeless and
care for the
young

THE KINGDOM

So near and yet still so far, far away
So close, and yet still to come
Concealed, the seed is mysteriously
    growing
In hearts that will listen and hear
A treasure that's hidden, a pearl of great
    price
A fortune for fools who believe

A kingdom of beauty, a kingdom of love
A kingdom of justice and peace
A kingdom that holds all the wilds of creation
A kingdom where children will lead[1]

For now this kingdom's a land of the lowly[2]
A place for the tired, plundered poor
Now our gentle King comes in peace on a
    donkey[3]
But then on a charger for war[4]
A battle in heaven, a war on the earth
To shatter the long darkened siege

Not by our own strength
And not by power of might[5]
But by His Spirit it comes
Blinded eyes will see
And deafened ears will hear [6]
The praise from the lips of the dumb

[1] Isaiah 11:6
[2] Ezekiel 29:14
[3] Zechariah 9:9
[4] Revelation 19:11
[5] Zechariah 4:6
[6] Isaiah 29:18; 35:15

The kingdom of God exists as the "now" and the "not yet." Though they are both the same kingdom, they could not seem more dissimilar. The kingdom of the now, over which Jesus reigns, is a hidden kingdom, a lowly land. Its inhabitants are weak in the ways He was weak and strong in the ways He was strong. It is ruled by the weak and the fragile and the fallen, and a donkey-mounted, lowly King.

The kingdom that is not yet—but is soon to come—is an unimaginably beautiful and powerful place. Its king, the same Jesus, rides on a white war horse and comes in unspeakable strength.

Both are ruled by the King. Both the same kingdom. But the world can scarcely grasp that they are one.

so near
AND YET STILL SO FAR
F A R   A   W A Y
so close
AND YET STILL TO COME

concealed the seed is
mysteriously growing

IN HEARTS THAT WILL LISTEN AND HEAR

A TREASURE
THAT'S HIDDEN

a pearl of
great price

A Fortune

for
fools
who
believe